THE BIRTH OF DRAMA

Theater in Ancient Greece

by Miranda Spekes • illustrated by Daniel Powers

Chapters

The Theater	4
The Beginnings of Drama	8
The Actors	10
Tragedy and Comedy	14
What Happened to Greek Drama?	16
A Brief Drama Glossary	16

Harcourt

Orlando Boston Dallas Chicago San Diego

Visit *The Learning Site!*
www.harcourtschool.com

A large audience sits in an open-air theater, in the noisy calm before a play begins. The theater itself is shaped like an enormous bowl. Below the audience, at what would be the bowl's center, lies an empty, flat, round space. Fanning out in a semicircle around that space, climbing the hillside in row after row, are the seats, divided into a mosaic of sections that are somewhat wedge-shaped, like the slices of a half-eaten pie. There are thousands of people here, all of them talking quietly, waiting for the actors and the chorus to come out. The author of today's play is a popular writer, and the crowd is eager to see his latest work.

Suddenly a hush sweeps across the crowd as the actors enter and walk to the center of the stage . . .

More than 2,500 years have passed since Athenians sat in the open-air Theater of Dionysus to watch the first plays performed in ancient Greece. Though much about drama has remained the same over the centuries, much more has changed.

Even though a theater audience today may have an experience similar to that of a playgoer of ancient Athens—sometimes even seeing the same *plays* that playgoers saw back then—no one would ever confuse the two dramatic periods. Ancient Greek drama was very different from today's theater. Yet, the plays and stories from that distant era can act as a window into a bygone world to help us understand the origins of drama.

The theater described above, the Theater of Dionysus, is laid out in the typical Greek style. Today, most theaters still use this same layout.

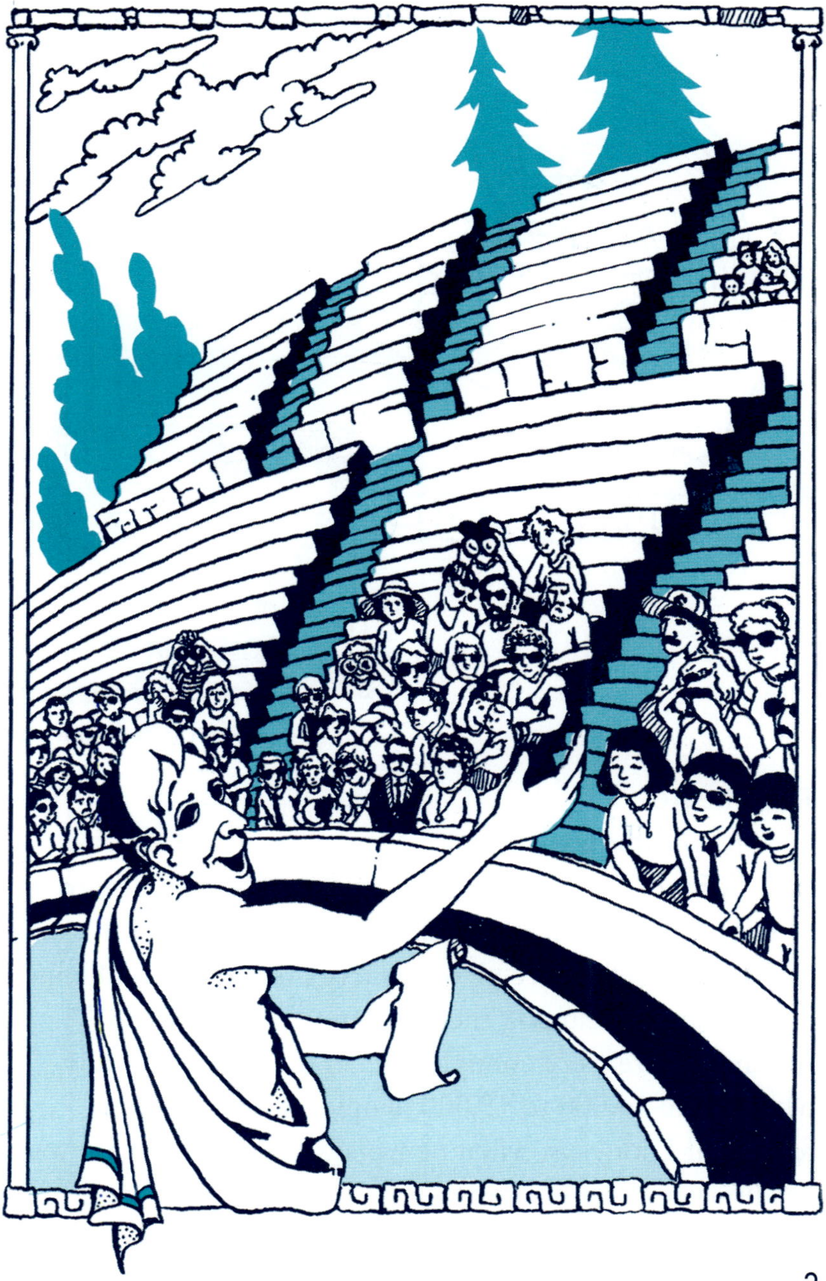

Theater of Dionysus

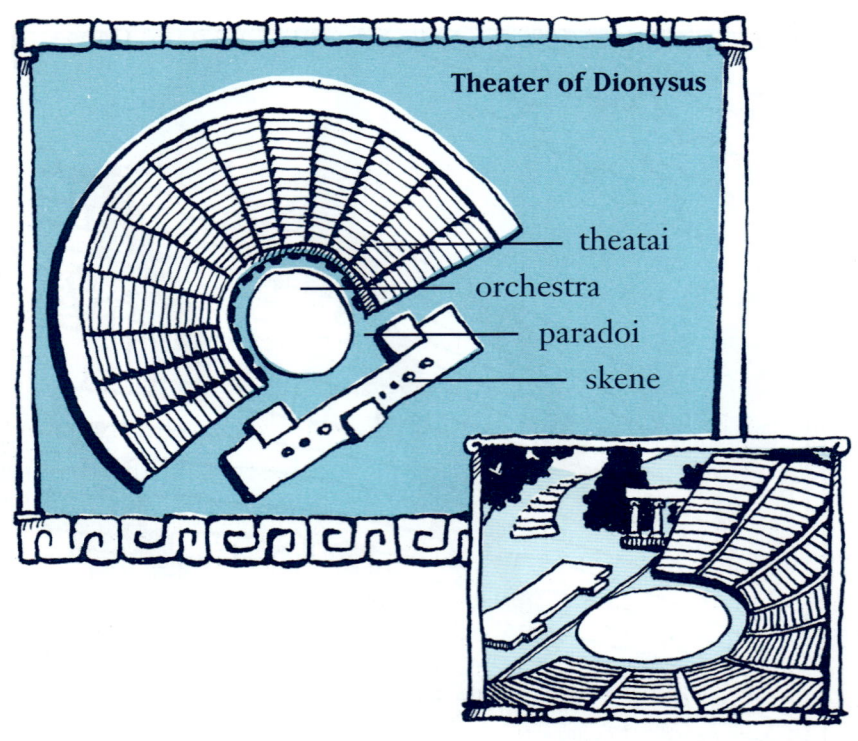

— theatai
— orchestra
— paradoi
— skene

Theater of Epidaurus

The Theater

The theater was an important part of life in Athens, and, fittingly, it was near the city's center. The Theater of Dionysus was cut into a hill beneath the Athenian Acropolis, a hill where all of the city's important buildings were located, including the Parthenon, the temple of Athena. There were enough seats in the theater for anywhere from 14,000 to 17,000 people, and during the festival of Dionysus, when new plays premiered, there was hardly ever an empty seat.

Typical Athenian theaters looked much like the one at Epidaurus, which is still in use today. The Theater of Dionysus no longer stands, but it is easy to see what it would have looked like from its ruins. If we were to reconstruct the Theater of Dionysus, we might expect it to look like the Epidaurus theater in the picture.

The audience sat in what was called the *theatai*, from which we get the word *theater*. The theatai was a semicircular set of benches, with aisles between sections. The audience faced a circular space called the *orchestra*, where the chorus performed. Between the orchestra and the theatai were the *paradoi*, passages that led to either side of the orchestra. The actors and the chorus walked down the paradoi at the beginning of the play.

Behind the orchestra was the *skene*, a long building that ran the full length of the orchestra. In the earliest dramas a speaker would stand on or near the skene and recite or sing a story. Meanwhile, on the orchestra floor in front of the speaker, the chorus would support the speaker with dances and songs. Later, as drama developed, the actors and the chorus played their parts together on the orchestra floor, while the skene became the place where the actors rested or went to switch costumes. Our word *scene* comes from the Greek word *skene*, since the breaks between acts were often signaled when the actors retreated into the skene to change costumes.

The basic setup of the Theater of Dionysus may resemble a modern theater, but the similarities end there. In the ancient Athenian theater, the plays began at dawn, lasted all day, and took place under the open sky. At lunchtime the audience might go home for a meal and a nap and then return in the afternoon for the rest of the show. Nowadays we tend to see plays performed indoors, lit by electric lights, and—unless we are attending a matinee—we attend the theater at night.

Athenians were hardly a polite audience, either. Today's theatergoers generally show respectful silence during a performance and then applaud at the end; by contrast, ancient Athenian audiences cheered, booed, and reacted loudly to every twist and turn of the play's story. The audience wasn't concerned about hygiene, as they sometimes even threw rotten food. This practice wasn't viewed as rude, but rather as one way a playgoer could vote against a play. Votes counted, because when drama first began, plays were part of an annual competition.

GREAT GREEK PLAYWRIGHTS

AESCHYLUS

Aeschylus (about 525–456 B.C.), the first of the great Greek tragic playwrights, was a nobleman who fought in the Persian Wars before becoming a poet and playwright. Aeschylus is often credited with creating the first real dramas, partly because his plays are the oldest surviving examples of Athenian tragedy. He was also the first to add a second actor, giving us the first examples of real dialogue between characters. Before his time plays had included only one actor and a chorus.

Of the eighty to ninety plays Aeschylus wrote, only seven survive. The most famous of these are *Oresteia: Agamemnon, The Libation Bearers,* and *The Furies.* The three plays that make up the *Oresteia* form a trilogy about the idea of justice and how it has evolved—from bloody revenge to punishment by the government. The *Oresteia* is still frequently staged today, as is another play by Aeschylus called *Prometheus Bound.*

The Beginnings of Drama

Athenian drama was born during annual festivals in honor of the Greek god Dionysus. At the festivals three playwrights competed, each with a set of four plays. This meant that the audience had to sit through a total of twelve plays before the competition could be decided.

Each playwright was required to present three tragedies focusing on a theme—a trilogy that would explore an idea in several different ways. After the last play in the trilogy ended, the writer had to entertain the audience with a comic fourth play, called a *satyr play*. The satyr play had the same theme as the dramatic trilogy, but it made fun of the trilogy and lightened everyone's mood. The idea was that the satyr play would cheer up the audience and send them home on a happy note.

The earliest plays featured a speaker and a chorus of fifteen men. The speaker told a story, and the chorus danced and sang, filling in some parts of the story and also commenting on the story itself. These early "plays" weren't what a modern audience would recognize as *drama*. They were more like someone's reciting and singing a poem with a chorus as a backup. Often the speaker and the writer were the same person.

GREAT GREEK PLAYWRIGHTS

SOPHOCLES

Sophocles (*about* 496–406 B.C.) is considered the second great writer of Greek tragic drama. Sophocles came from a wealthy family and was very handsome, well educated, and popular. In addition to writing plays, he held one of the highest elected offices in Athens.

Sophocles wrote more than 120 plays. Of those, only seven remain, including *Oedipus the King* and *Antigone*. He won twenty-four dramatic contests, more than any other Athenian playwright. Not only was Sophocles a master of story, character, and poetic form, but he also changed Athenian drama by introducing a third actor to the plays. This feature allowed stories to be much more complex than before. Sophocles also reduced the role of the chorus and added realistic scenery to the stage.

Sophocles was a favorite of both audiences and critics. Perhaps what made his plays so popular were his down-to-earth characters. Unlike the larger-than-life heroes of Aeschylus, Sophocles' characters seem like real people. Their troubles and conflicts have less to do with mythology than with their human strengths and weaknesses.

The earliest drama on record was performed at a tragedy contest held in 534 B.C. The winner was a playwright and actor named Thespis. From his name we get the word *thespian*, meaning "actor," because, starting with Thespis the acting profession was born. Thespis had the idea of making one member of the chorus stand apart and engage in a kind of dialogue with the chorus. Dialogue made the storytelling at the festivals more dynamic and gave rise to the idea of a *drama*, in which characters enact a story. Plays could now *show* the story through actors speaking to one another and having conflicts with each other. The playwright Aeschylus added a second actor, and eventually three actors performed in front of the chorus.

The Actors

Actors weren't the only performers in Greek theater. There were also the members of the chorus and the musicians. Performers were always men, because the Greeks considered acting an inappropriate activity for women. The absence of women didn't restrict playwrights, however, because all actors wore masks while onstage. An actor could play the part of a female by donning women's clothing and a wigged mask.

GREAT GREEK PLAYWRIGHTS

EURIPIDES

Euripides (about 480–406 B.C.) was the last of the three great Greek writers of tragedy. He was also the least popular of the three during his lifetime, because the themes of his plays made many Athenians uncomfortable.

For example, his play *Helen,* about what happened to Helen of Troy *after* the Trojan War, looks at the human cost of war and reveals Euripides' hatred of warfare. In all, Euripides wrote some ninety plays, eighteen of which survive. He also wrote the only surviving satyr play. Several of Euripides' plays, such as *Electra* and *The Trojan Women*, are still staged today, perhaps because his stories are complex enough to appeal to modern audiences.

The actors' masks accomplished two things. First, they allowed the playwrights to write stories with more than three characters. The rules of the competition said that each playwright could use only three actors. In order to portray all of the characters in a play, the actors had to make frequent character and costume changes. By taking off one mask and pulling on another, an actor could play the parts of male and female characters of any age, or even of animals. Second, the masks, with their large mouths and eyes and exaggerated expressions, were easy to see even for the person sitting farthest away in the audience. (Today actors still exaggerate their features with makeup so their faces will be visible to even the most distant members of the audience.)

Greek actors went through rigorous training, just like athletes. An actor's voice had to be strong and musical, so everyone in the audience could understand him even through his mask. The costumes were physically demanding, too. Actors wore stilt-like boots in addition to their masks, and they had to sing and dance for hours while in costume. To prepare, actors and choruses rehearsed together for as much as eight months before a festival.

GREAT GREEK PLAYWRIGHTS

ARISTOPHANES

Aristophanes (about 448–388 B.C.), one of the great writers of ancient Greek comedy, is the only comic playwright whose plays have survived. Eleven of his forty plays remain, among them *The Clouds*, *The Frogs*, and *Lysistrata*. Aristophanes' plays are satires; they include a mix of beautiful poetry, side-splitting farce, savage wit, parody, serious observations of his society, and jabs at other playwrights and public figures, as well as dance and song. No one escaped Aristophanes' wit, not even dead playwrights! In his play *The Frogs*, the god Dionysus, dissatisfied with theater after the death of Euripides, descends into the underworld to bring Euripides back. There he finds Euripides and Aeschylus insulting each other's work.

Tragedy and Comedy

Thespis wrote *tragedy*, the first form of Greek drama. Later, *comedy* was added to the Dionysian festivals. The traditional masks of the theater—a frowning mask and a grinning mask—are emblems of these two kinds of ancient drama. They are a direct reference to the masks actors wore in Greek tragedies and comedies.

Some tragedies told stories of the gods and their relationships with human characters; they often ended unhappily. Gods in Greek stories were not all-powerful, mysterious beings who knew everything; they had human faults and emotions, and they often made mistakes.

Sometimes humans suffered because of a god's misbehavior, but people also had free will in these plays.

Other tragedies retold stories that the audience already knew, stories of heroes struggling with destiny. These tales focused on characters, such as Agamemnon or Helen of Troy, who were familiar to the audiences from legends, history, and artwork such as paintings and mosaics. These plays added a human dimension to larger-than-life figures.

Comedies were quite different from tragedies. Instead of a fifteen-member chorus, comedic choruses had as many as twenty-four people. Sometimes the chorus portrayed nonhuman things or animals, such as clouds or frogs. What's more, comedies had very different subject matter from tragedies. Instead of gods and legendary men and women, comedies depicted contemporary events and people—often public figures whom the audience knew very well. Comedic playwrights used their plays to comment on and poke fun at politics and art or to settle scores with people who had displeased them. Because comedic plays were often merciless and unkind, their performances usually occurred during winter festivals, when few visitors from other provinces would be in town to see the locals embarrassed and laughed at.

Eventually two yearly festivals—one for comedy and one for tragedy—became a tradition in Athens. During the rest of the year, festival actors toured Greece, performing for people in the provinces all over the country.

What Happened to Greek Drama?

Greek drama was old by the time the young Roman Empire made Greece a province around 146 B.C. The Romans liked Greek theater so much that they brought it home. Like many things the Romans took from others, such as the aqueduct, they changed Greek drama. The Romans made drama less complex. Greek plays were intended to entertain but also to make the audience *think*. Roman plays, on the other hand, were geared more for simple entertainment. With the start of the Roman Empire, the golden age of Greek drama came to an end.

A Brief Drama Glossary

chorus	a group of fifteen to twenty-four performers who danced, sang, took part in a drama, and commented on it
comedy	drama that satirized contemporary events and people
orchestra	a circular area on which the chorus and actors performed the play
skene	the structure at the back of the stage in which actors could rest or change costumes; origin of the word *scene*
theatai	the area in an ancient theater where the audience sat; origin of the word *theater*
thespian	actor (derived from *Thespis*, the first known actor/playwright)
tragedy	a drama about gods and heroes that often ended unhappily